Project Management: The Sketches

by

Nigel Creaser

<Project Management: The Sketches> / Script / 3

All characters are fictitious and in no way represent anyone I have had the pleasure of working with. Any offence caused to any profession is entirely intentional, and really you should take a good long hard look at yourself and lighten up a bit, this is meant to be funny. Please note all typorgaphical ererrs our all my own werk.

Your Reading Backlog

One

Kinds of Lies

SCENE: George Onaswell, presses the play symbol on his brand new Narkia N95 phone, the dulcet tones of Kirsty Wright flow through his headphone, only the left one is in his ear.

KIRSTY:

We introduce Benjamin Disraeli, PM and not Prime Minister, the usual meaning for the post-nominal letters. It is a little known fact that it actually stood for Project Manager, oft-debated by historians, but I think the evidence is compelling. In an interview with Mark Twain, for his popular video blog, "Life After Huckleberry: A Wanderers Tale" they discuss project management topics, here is a recently discovered transcript of the interview.

TWAIN

Benji, thanks for making time for the interview today.

DISRAELI

You're welcome Marky baby, good to talk about Project Management for a change, instead of all that running a country stuff, borrrring.

TWAIN

So I wanted to talk to you about truth in project management. What are your views?

DISRAELI

Well you see I believe there are 3 kinds of lies in this arena "Lies, Damn Lies and Statistics."

TWAIN

That's interesting, so how about some examples?

DISRAELI

Yea sure. Let's take Lies first, you know when you ask one of the team will we hit the date for such and such and they say "Yea should be OK!"

TWAIN

Oh yea we all heard that one, that should word is massive in that sentence.

DISRAELI

Damn lies where we ask "Did you test that bit?" about something is not working and you get "Yes" they say and then quietly or later on add "Well it worked on my machine yesterday"

TWAIN

Man I hate that, makes me wanna scream.

DISRAELI

And of course the biggest of them all, statistics! Velocity, earned value, defect fix rates per day, hour or minute, they can all say what you want. You just, change the % of or absolute number, or do a fancy graph that no one understands.

TWAIN

> OK, so we have the three of them then, but what about project plans?

DISRAELI

> Well that's a good point most of them are a bit flaky so yes I would say there are 4 kinds of lies "Lies, Damn Lies, Statistics and Project Plans!"

TWAIN

> So you would say that covers the lot then?

DISRAELI

> Yes, I think so, oh hang there estimating as well. So there are yes five kind of lies in project management "Lies, Damn Lies, Statistics, Project Plans and Estimates"

TWAIN

> Of course its all that "contingency" people add in for risks that might happen. Eh?

DISRAELI

> Damn!

TWAIN

> What?

DISRAELI

> I forgot risk mitigation plans, no one has much
> of a risk mitigation plan that stands up to much
> scrutiny, just a wing and a prayer.

TWAIN

> So that makes six then?

DISRAELI

> Yes there are six kinds of lies in project
> management "Lies, Damn Lies, Statistics, Project
> Plans, Estimates and Risk Mitigation Plans"

TWAIN

> Makes up most of the components of the projects
> reporting then.

DISRAELI

> Arghhh! Project Status Reports!

TWAIN

> Oh! Another one?

DISRAELI

> Uhu! So there's, let me count 1, 2, 3, 4, 5, 6, 7,
> yes, seven kinds of lies in project management.
> "Lies, Damn Lies, Statistics, Project Plans,
> Estimates, Risk Mitigation Plans and Project
> Status Reports"

TWAIN

> Brilliant! Thank you for your wonderful insight. Hey I know you are a busy man with all that running a country business, so I will let you get on with your day. And Thanks again Benji.

DISRAELI

> No problem, thanks for having me on your show, really enjoyed it.

TWAIN

> Right all that leaves now, is for me to trail next week's show where Hannibal will be talking about how you get approval to buy a whole load of elephants and march them over the Pyrenees with just a four page business case.

DISRAELI

> Bollocks, business cases, aaaaaaaahhhhhhhhh!

TWAIN

> Ehm! OK, see you all next week. [*To DISRAELI*] Benji, are you OK?.....

Two

The Holy Grail of Extra Funding

SCENE: The bitter battle sounds of an argument around the quality of the documentation being handed over for final acceptance into live. The Green Knight Project Manager completes another difficult project in a bloody project lessons learned meeting as Arthur watches.

ARTHUR:
> You negotiate with the resilience of 100 hostage negotiators, Sir Knight PM.
>
> *[pause]*
>
> I am Arthur, King of the of the Grunnlings Assorted Fixings (est. 1843) Ltd PMO (est. 2003)
>
> *[pause]*
>
> I seek the finest and the bravest project managers in the land to join me in my Grunnlings Assorted Fixings (est. 1843) Ltd PMO (est. 2003) in my quest to find the Holy Grail of Extra Funding.
>
> *[pause]*
>
> You have proved yourself worthy; will you join me? Though to do so you will obviously need to change your RAG status to Red.
>
> *[The GREEN KNIGHT PM just makes a gentle, but firm shake of his helmeted head]*
>
> You make me sad. So be it. Come, Lancelot.

GREEN KNIGHT PM:
> The project is green.

ARTHUR:
> What?

GREEN KNIGHT PM:
> The project is green.

ARTHUR:
> I have no quarrel with you, good sir knight, but
> I must set the RAG to Red.

GREEN KNIGHT PM:
> Then you shall die.

ARTHUR:
> I command you as King of the Grunnlings
> Assorted Fixings (est. 1843) Ltd PMO (est. 2003)
> to set your status to Red!

GREEN KNIGHT PM:
> I move for no stakeholder, nor sponsor, no
> matter how high their seniority, influence or
> executive bathroom access.

ARTHUR:
> So be it! [hah]
> [emails sent, parry thrust. ARTHUR chops the
> GREEN KNIGHT PM's initial funding off after a
> short business case review]

ARTHUR:
> Now stand, change your RAG and submit your go
> to green, worthy adversary.

GREEN KNIGHT PM:
> 'Tis causing but a minor slippage. We will still
> hit the date.

ARTHUR:
> A minor slippage? Your funding has gone!

GREEN KNIGHT PM:
> Not all of it, it isn't.

ARTHUR:
> *[Pointing at the latest funding allocation dashboard on the 77 inch 4k curved LED screen that dominates the main office of the Grunnlings Assorted Fixings (est. 1843) Ltd PMO (est. 2003)]*
>
> Well, what's that then?

GREEN KNIGHT PM:
> I've had worse funding problems. I have some savings tucked away from the first phase.

ARTHUR:
> You liar! It's just like one of your progress reports.

GREEN KNIGHT PM:
> Come on you wimp! I'll 'ave you for that, questioning my honesty, would ya? Eh? *[hah]*
> *[Parry thrust latest project progress report, ARTHUR sends all of the GREEN KNIGHT PM's resources on corporate social responsibility duties for the next month]*

ARTHUR:

> Victory is mine! *[kneeling]* We thank thee great
> Project Sponsor in the sky, that in thy merc-
> *[The GREEN KNIGHT PM throws a pack of Agile
> estimation cards at Arthur's head while he is
> praying]*

GREEN KNIGHT PM:

> Come an 'ave a go then.

ARTHUR:

> What?

GREEN KNIGHT PM:

> Come an 'ave a go then! I have a bunch of interns
> and school work experience kids on the main UX
> phase! They are all much more with this social
> media generation X user stuff anyway so should
> deliver it quicker too with better quality.

ARTHUR:

> You are brave, Sir PM, but the fight is mine.
> Even with your whizzy UX phase the core
> integration phase is laggin' behind and you
> have no money or team to rescue it.
> *[Arthur turns to leave]*

GREEN KNIGHT PM:

> Ah you have finally accepted I have a green
> status have ya?

ARTHUR:
>Look, you stupid git, you've got no funding or
>team left.

GREEN KNIGHT PM:
>I have enough I have got my interns.

ARTHUR:
>Look!
>
>*[Arthur shows the GREEN KNIGHT PM the latest
>resource and funding allocation report.]*

GREEN KNIGHT PM:
>Just a minor hiccup. Nothing a bit of risk
>mitigation planning won't solve.
>
>*[Pulls out a copy of The Risk Management
>Handbook: A Practical Guide to Managing the
>Multiple Dimensions of Risk by Dr David
>Hillson (available at this link) and waves it in
>Arthur's face.]*

ARTHUR:
>Look, stop that.

GREEN KNIGHT PM:
>Coward! Big scaredy coward.

ARTHUR:
>Look, I'll have your timeline halved. Right!
>[whop]

GREEN KNIGHT PM:
>Right, I'll smash your face in for that! And still
>deliver the project with one hand.

ARTHUR:

You'll what? What will you use a time machine?

GREEN KNIGHT PM:

Come 'ere! I 'll just get more interns and renegotiate the benefits case for the big-ticket items.

ARTHUR:

What are you going to do, the old get nine women to have a baby in one month, trick eh?

GREEN KNIGHT PM:

I'm an invincible internationally certified project professional! I meet all the three points of project management triangle, time, cost and quality.

ARTHUR:

You're certifiable alright!

GREEN KNIGHT PM:

The Green Knight PM always delivers on time, to budget and scope! Have at you! Come on then.

[Whop ARTHUR doubles the GREEN KNIGHT PM's product backlog]

GREEN KNIGHT PM:

All right; we'll call it Amber.

ARTHUR:

Come, Lancelot.

GREEN KNIGHT PM:
> Oh, oh, I see, running away, 'eh? ... You cowardly
> blighters! ... I'll change control your product
> backlog items up your own jacksie!

Three

I like RAG Status

SCENE: The favourite song of Arthur, King of the Grunnlings Assorted Fixings (est. 1843) Ltd PMO (est. 2003) is played continuously throughout offices over the latest [*Product placement opportunity!! Please email sundaylunchpm@gmail.com to advertise here*] voice assistant speakers.

To recreate that atmosphere please sing this in as monotone a voice as you can manage, if you are an eternally upbeat person, please ask your most boring colleague to sing it for you.

I like RAG Status

I like RAG status,

I like RAG status,

I like RAG status,

I hope by RAG you know what I mean.

I like RAG status,

I like RAG status,

I like RAG status,

I like RAG status,

But only when they're green.

He likes RAG status,

He likes RAG status,

He likes RAG status,

He likes RAG status,

If you know what I mean.

He likes RAG status,

He likes RAG status,

He likes RAG status,

But only when they're green.

I like RAG status,

I like RAG status,

I like RAG status,

Though I sing like I am dead.

I like RAG status,

I like RAG status,

I like RAG status,

But not when they are red.

He likes RAG status,

He likes RAG status,

He likes RAG status,

Though he sings like he is dead.

He likes RAG status,

He likes RAG status,

He likes RAG status,

He likes RAG status,

Especially when they are orange.

I like RAG status,

I like RAG status,

I like RAG status,

I like RAG status,

I like RAG status,

I like RAG status,

I like RAG status,

I like RAG status,

I like RAG status,

But can think of something to rhyme with orange

He likes RAG status,

He likes RAG status,

He likes RAG status,

He likes RAG status,

He likes RAG status,

But not when they are amber.

I like RAG status,

I like RAG status,

I like RAG status,

Although my name's not Bamber.

I like RAG status,

I like RAG status,

I like RAG status,

I...Oh God!

Four

Blasphemy!!!! he said Contingency

SCENE: Our hero, Junior Developer George Onaswell who is curious about the romantic notion of project management and doesn't want to just keep on following in the footsteps of his current mentor Merv, the senior engineer. Merv, at Georges request is sneaking George into one of the hallowed grounds of a project review in the PMO at Grunnlings Assorted Fixings (est. 1843) Ltd.

SENIOR ENGINEER MERV:

Ah, I really hate wearing these beards.

DEVELOPER GEORGE:

Why aren't developers allowed to go to projects reviews, Merv?

SENIOR ENGINEER MERV:

It's written that's why.

DEVELOPER GEORGE:

Where is it written Merv?

SENIOR ENGINEER MERV:

Why, it's written in the good book.

DEVELOPER GEORGE:

Ahhh! *[Long Pause]*.....err? which book is that then?

SENIOR ENGINEER MERV:

The Scrum Guide I think, or some *[Joey air quotes]* "Body of Knowledge" book.... or was it the governance plan thingy, I don't know, you know these bloody Project Managers and their documents, probably in all of them worded slightly different.

BEARD/REPORT SELLER:

Pssst! Beard, madam?

DEVELOPER *[carrying a progress report]***:**

Oh, look, I haven't got the time to go the project review. I need to get on and do the work not spend all my time reporting on it.

DONKEY:

Woof! Woof!

BEARD AND REPORT SELLER:

Progress Report, sir?

SENIOR ENGINEER MERV:

No, they've got a lot lying around by the printer over there

BEARD AND REPORT SELLER:

Oh, not like these, sir. Look at this! Look at the quality of that, that's craftsmanship, sir. See the different RAG status colours? That's all done automatically with conditional formatting, none of you manual colour coding here.

SENIOR ENGINEER MERV:

Hmm...all right, we'll have two with and...a Gantt chart too.

DEVELOPER GEORGE:

Could I have a Gantt chart too, senior Engineer Merv?

SENIOR ENGINEER MERV:

Ssch!

DEVELOPER GEORGE:

Sorry! Senior 'Project Manager' Merv!

SENIOR ENGINEER MERV:

> Ehm...all right, two progress reports, two Gantt charts and ahm...a list of un-approved change requests, they're usually quite weighty.

BEARD AND REPORT SELLER:

> List of assumptions. Should be a good one today.

SENIOR ENGINEER MERV:

> How come?

BEARD AND REPORT SELLER:

> Permanent boy, next office down.

SENIOR ENGINEER MERV:

> Good, that a make change from all these bloody contractors that seem to around these days, always banging on about IR35.

BEARD AND REPORT SELLER:

> Have a nice day, y'all!

DEVELOPER GEORGE:

> Weird, he did not have a Deep South American accent before.

SENIOR ENGINEER MERV:

> Dunno, maybe its all them new-fangled voice assistants with their funny voices. Perhaps he his trying to get in the act of being more global?

DEVELOPERS DISGUISED AS PROJECT MANAGERS:

> [Screaming and yelling]

PETERS (HEAD OF PLANNING COMPLIANCE):

Matthews, Project Manager of Project of Decentralisation of Grunnlings Assorted Fixings (est. 1843) dist...

MATTHEWS:

Do I say yes?

GUARD:

Yes.

MATTHEWS:

Yes!

PETERS:

...you have been found guilty by the Programme and Portfolio Managers of the PMO of uttering blasphemy...

DEVELOPERS DISGUISED AS PROJECT MANAGERS:

Ooh...

PETERS:

...you are sentenced to a death of a thousand progress report paper cuts!

DEVELOPERS DISGUISED AS PROJECT MANAGERS:

Aah!

MATTHEWS:

Look, I'd had a lovely plan review, and all I said to my Project Analyst was: "That estimate for that piece of work needs some Contingency!".

DEVELOPERS DISGUISED AS PROJECT MANAGERS:

Oooh!

PETERS:

>   Blasphemy! He said it again!

DEVELOPERS DISGUISED AS PROJECT MANAGERS:

>   Yeah! Yes! Yes!

PETERS:

>   Did you hear him?!

DEVELOPERS DISGUISED AS PROJECT MANAGERS:

>   Yeah! Yes!

DEVELOPER DISGUISED AS A PROJECT MANAGER WEARING PENGUIN CUFFLINKS:

>   Shut down his GitHub account!

PETERS:

>   Are there any developers today?

DEVELOPERS DISGUISED AS PROJECT MANAGERS:

>   Uh...ooh...no.. *[penguin   cufflinks   hastily covered up]*

PETERS:

>   Very well. By virtue of the authority vested in me as set out in the portfolio charter...

PROGRESS REPORT FOLDED IN THE SHAPE OF A PAPER AEROPLANE THROWN AT MATTHEWS:

>   *[Zoom, zoom, flutter crunch]*

DEVELOPERS DISGUISED AS PROJECT MANAGERS:

>   Ooh...

MATTHEWS:

> Oh, lay off! We haven't started yet! Could have had my eye out.

PETERS:

> Come on! Who threw that? Who threw that report? Come on!

DEVELOPERS DISGUISED AS PROJECT MANAGERS:

> Java Jen did! Java Jen did! Java Jen did! PM Jen did! PM Jen did!

JAVA JEN:

> Sorry, I thought we'd started.

PETERS [shaking his head watching Java Jen walk to the back]:

> You! Go to the back! Go on!

DEVELOPER:

> Oh, dear...

PETERS:

> Always one, isn't there? Now, where was I?

MATTHEWS:

> Look, you can't call it blasphemy, just for saying "Contingency"!

DEVELOPERS DISGUISED AS PROJECT MANAGERS:

> Oiiii! He said it again!

PETERS:

> You're only making it worse for yourself!

MATTHEWS:

> Making it worse? How in the PMO head's name could it be worse? I'll shout it from the rooftops, what ya gonna do, kill me even more? CONTINGENCY, CONTINGENCY, CONTINGENCY!

DEVELOPERS DISGUISED AS PROJECT MANAGERS:

> Aiiih!

PETERS:

> I'm warning you! If you say Contingency once more...

REPORT THROWN AT PETERS:

> Flutter.

PETERS:

> Right! Who threw that?

MATTHEWS:

> Hehehe...

PETERS:

> Come on! Who threw that?

DEVELOPERS DISGUISED AS PROJECT MANAGERS:

> Python Paul! Python Paul! Python Paul! PM Paul! PM Paul! PM Paul!

PETERS:

> Was it you?

PYTHON PAUL:

> Yes.

PETERS:

> Right...

PYTHON PAUL:

Well, you did say Contingency!

DEVELOPERS DISGUISED AS PROJECT MANAGERS:

Aiiih!

REPORTS THROWN AT PYTHON PAUL:

Multiple flutters.

PETERS:

Stop it! Stop it! Will you cease and desist, stop that! Stop now! Now, look! No one is to paper cut anyone until I approve this project initiation document! Do you understand? Even, and I want to make this absolutely bloody clear as the clearest scope statement, even if they do say Contingency!

DEVELOPERS DISGUISED AS PROJECT MANAGERS:

Yea! Get him! Yeaaaaaah!

REPORTS THROWN AT PETERS:

Multiple flutters

PETERS:

Aaargh!

AN INCONCEIVABLY LARGE REAM OF REPORTS FALLS FROM THE SKY CRUSHING PETERS:

Massive flutters.

DEVELOPER III: DEVELOPERS DISGUISED AS PROJECT MANAGERS:
Good shot!
[Applause, cheer, much back slapping]

Matthews, as sneaky as a sneaky thing, carefully slips away, past the bloody, paper cut corpse of Peters.

Five

Scrum

SCENE: The reception area in the Grunnlings Assorted Fixing (est. 1843) Ltd, Project Management Office (est. 2003). Reception seating is occupied by a group of Java Developers with horned helmets on. Only one table is free. Jessica Blenkinsop, Project Manager, and her newly appointed Project Analyst George Onaswell enter.

JESSICA:

Grab us a seat George.

GEORGE:

All right.

PROJECT MANAGER *[to receptionist]*:

Morning!

RECEPTIONIST:

Morning!

JESSICA:

I have just been given my new project, what have you got for us to manage it with?

RECEPTIONIST [*Pointing at the black pin board with gold lettering*]:

Well, [*BIG BREATH*] there's

waterfall and lean;

waterfall, agile and lean;

waterfall and Scrum;

waterfall, lean and Scrum;

waterfall, lean, agile and Scrum;

Scrum, lean, agile and Scrum;

Scrum, waterfall, Scrum, Scrum, lean and Scrum;

Scrum, agile, Scrum, Scrum, lean, Scrum, Kaizen and Scrum;

JAVA DEVELOPERS [*starting to chant*]:

Scrum, Scrum, Scrum, Scrum...

RECEPTIONIST *[still on the same breath]*:

> ...Scrum, Scrum, Scrum, waterfall and Scrum; Scrum, Scrum, Scrum, Scrum, Scrum, Scrum, baked beans, Scrum, Scrum, Scrum...

JAVA DEVELOPERS *[singing]*:

> Scrum! Lovely Scrum! Lovely Scrum!

JESSICA:

> Baked beans?

RECEPTIONIST:

> Sorry, that's wrong, let me just check, [long pause as receptionist checks computer, writes down reference from the computer onto a sticky note, takes a pair of white cotton gloves from one of the desk drawers and turns to pull a large brown leather book from its case. Down the spine large golden Times New Roman lettering, its name is embossed ... THE BODY OF KNOWLEDGE.

> Unlocking each of the locks and with great care he places the book in front of him. As if touching butterfly wings, he cautiously turns the pages until he reaches a page at the back, notes something on the sticky, the with similar care back towards the front, again taking a note, and then finally to the middle of the book.

He reverently closes the tome and with
excruciating care places it back in its case,
locking it away and places the gloves back in
their home, and looks up to the Project Manager]

RECEPTIONIST:

.....yeah, thought so, that should be Scrum.

JESSICA:

Stares agog at the receptionist

RECEPTIONIST:

...or SDLC with a smattering of XP, delivered in
Six Sigma manner with RUP and RAD interlaced
with Kaizen on top and Scrum.

GEORGE:

Have you got anything without Scrum?

RECEPTIONIST:

Well, there's Scrum, waterfall, agile and Scrum,
that's not got much Scrum in it.

GEORGE:

I don't want ANY Scrum!

JESSICA:

Why can't he have waterfall lean Scrum and
agile?

GEORGE:

THAT'S got Scrum in it!

JESSICA:

> Hasn't got as much Scrum in it as Scrum waterfall agile and Scrum, has it?

JAVA DEVELOPERS:

> Scrum, Scrum, Scrum, Scrum *[crescendo through next few lines]*

GEORGE:

> Could you do the waterfall lean Scrum and agile without the Scrum then?

RECEPTIONIST:

> Yuk!

GEORGE:

> What do you mean 'Yuk'? I just don't like Scrum!

JAVA DEVELOPERS:

> Lovely Scrum! Wonderful Scrum!

RECEPTIONIST:

> Shut up you lot!

JAVA DEVELOPERS:

> Lovely Scrum! Wonderful Scrum!

RECEPTIONIST:

> I said shut up! *[JAVA DEVELOPERS stop]* Bloody Java Developers! You can't have waterfall lean Scrum and agile without the Scrum.

GEORGE *[shrieks]***:**

> I don't like Scrum!

JESSICA *[in a whisper to GEORGE]*:
Sshh, don't cause a fuss. I'll have your Scrum. As long as we stand up for 15 minutes each morning people will think we are doing Scrum, and get one of them Kanban boards, it'll be fine. I love it.

JESSICA to RECEPTIONIST
I'm having Scrum, Scrum, Scrum, Scrum, Scrum, Scrum, Scrum, Kanban, Scrum, Scrum, Scrum, and Scrum!

JAVA DEVELOPERS *[singing]*:
Scrum, Scrum, Scrum, Scrum. Lovely Scrum! Wonderful Scrum!

RECEPTIONIST:
Shut up!! Kanban is off. We run out of sticky notes.

JESSICA:
Well could I have his Scrum instead of the Kanban then?

RECEPTIONIST:
You mean Scrum, Scrum, Scrum, Scrum, Scrum, Scrum... *[but it is too late and the JAVA DEVELOPERS drown her words]*

JAVA DEVELOPERS *[singing elaborately]*:
Scrum, Scrum, Scrum, Scrum.
Lovely Scrum!
Wonderful Scrum! Scrum, Scr-r-r-r-r-um,
Scrum, Scr-r-r-r-r-um, Scrum.
Lovely Scrum!
Lovely Scrum!
Lovely Scrum!
Lovely Scrum!
Lovely Scrum!
Scrum, Scrum, Scrum, Scrum!

Six

The Professional Bodies

SCENE: The Excel Centre London, scene of ProManComCon, the UK's largest combined project management and comic book conference/convention. A rather harassed looking man, stands to the side of the main auditorium stage, his eyes darting from left to right, like a caged animal, seeking out a way of escape.

Another man dressed in a what was once perhaps a smart and fashionable suit. It has now seen better days having spent much of its time hanging off the back of a poorly set up office chair. He stands staring hard at the notes held in his shaking hands, trying desperately to focus on them, as he gently places them on the lavish, beech veneered lecture from 1973, which stands grandly in front of him.

SPEAKER:

Ladies and gentlemen! Please welcome our keynote speaker for this mornings breakfast briefing, Mr Peter Taylor, talking to us about" How not to get fired while being a Lazy Project Manager" I hope I don't get fired for being lazy conference host.

[A few murmurs of laughter dot the hungover audience, desperately waiting for the coffee to kick in and hope their boss sat next to them does not notice their eyelids closing and opening like the mouth of a hungry hippo.

To the side of the main auditorium, George, our hero wannabe Junior Project Manager, currently working at Listo Para Comer, a Spanish tapas, slash coffee shop, slash welding supplies, allowing him to get some extra cash and pick up some tips from the amassed project management community.

We join him as he finishes serving his latest victim slash customer.]

GEORGE:

Ah, right, thank you, madam.
[George turns to the crowd in general, trying to sound enthusiastic about his fare, but failing spectacularly]

GEORGE:

Get your gluten-free, dairy-free, egg-free, nut-free, sugar-free, meat and vegetable-free SpiegelDollen cake. How about partly sprouted frozen pea lumps. Try our limited edition coffee with grinds from beans filtered through the bowels of rare heritage pigs in Seville the famous PigDungCoffee. Slightly cloudy water filtered through the mountains of East Anglian! Erh? Stinky bishop, watercress and wild garlic flower quinoa crunchies!

[After suppressing his gag reflex, George deftly wigs his ear towards the conversation he notices on the upper tiers of the auditorium.

A group of shady looking characters had placed themselves in a position that spoke to their experience. Sat confident in the knowledge they are far enough away that the would have no chance of hearing the keynote speech, but would still appear to have been in attendance when submitting their grossly overestimated expenses later that week.]

JUDITH:

I do feel Jools, that any pro-traditional waterfall group like ours must reflect such a divergence of interest within its powerbase

JOOLS:

Agreed. Rogers?

ROGERS:

Yes, I think Judith's point of view is very valid, Jools, provided the movement never forgets that it is the sponsor given right of every Project Manager...

STAN:

Or Scrum Master.

ROGERS:

...or Scrum Master to rid scope...

STAN:

Or product backlog.

ROGERS:

...or, or product backlog...

JOOLS:

Agreed.

ROGERS:

Thank you, Um? What was I saying?

JOOLS:

Pretty sure you had finished.

ROGERS:

> Oh? OK? Could have swore I was gonna say something else.

JOOLS:

> Furthermore, it is the Certified right of every PM..

STAN:

> Or PSM/CSM.

JOOLS:

> Why don't you shut up about this Scrum stuff, Stan? You're putting us off.

STAN:

> Scrum Masters have a perfect right to play a part in our movement, Jools.

ROGERS:

> Why are you always on about Scrum Masters, Stan?

STAN:

> I want to be one.

JOOLS:

> What the f...?

STAN:

> I want to be a Scrum Master. From now on, I want you all to call me Stan The Scrum.

JOOLS:

> What the f...?

STAN THE SCRUM:

> It's my right as a Project Manager.

JUDITH:

> Well, why do you want to be Stan The Scrum, Stan?

STAN THE SCRUM:

> I want to do retrospectives.

JOOLS:

> You want do retrospectives?!

STAN THE SCRUM:

> It's every project manager's right to have retrospectives if he wants them.

JOOLS:

> But...you can't have retrospectives!

STAN THE SCRUM:

> Don't you oppress me!

JOOLS:

> I'm not oppressing you, Stan. You haven't got a product backlog or a sprint backlog, or a sprint for that matter. This is a waterfall project group, what are you going to retrospect in your retrospective?

STAN THE SCRUM:

> Sniff.

JUDITH:

> Here, I've got an idea. Suppose you agree that he can't actually have a retrospective, not having a sprint, which is nobody's fault, not even the line managers', but that he can have the right to have retrospective.

ROGERS:

> Good idea, Judith. We shall fight the oppressors for your right to have retrospectives, Stan. Stan the Scrum! Sorry.

JOOLS:

> What's the point?

ROGERS:

> What?

JOOLS:

What's the point of fighting for his right to have retrospectives, when he can't have retrospectives?

ROGERS:

It is symbolic of our struggle against

oppression.

JOOLS:

Symbolic of his struggle against reality. You might as well combine waterfall and Agile and call bloody WaterGile or AgiFall something just as daft.

TRUMPETS:

[Fanfares leading into a trumpet rendition of Lazy by Deep Purple]

AUDIENCE:

[Applause]

GUARD/COMPARE:

Get out there! Ah, get out there!

VICTIM (PETER TAYLOR):

I'm not going out there. Look at them they look nasty. It's dangerous out there! Aah! Aiih! Oh.

AUDIENCE:

We want lazy, we want lazy we want lazy.

VICTIM:

Listen to them, they want blood.

[George approaches the group of conspirators]

GEORGE:

Raw kale and mung bean chewies! Un-recyclable plastic pot of healthy stuff swimming in oil. Recyclable super quick biodegradable dolphin friendly pot of unhealthy stuff swimming in oil.

JOOLS:

Got any crisps?

GEORGE:

Haven't got any crisps, sorry. What about sprouted pea lumps, Peruvian grasshopper kidneys if coconut oil...

JOOLS:

No, no, no...

GEORGE:

Frozen Reykjavik salmon tears?

JOOLS:

> I don't want any of that stupid line management café rubbish!

JUDITH:

> Why don't you sell proper food?

GEORGE:

> Proper food?

JOOLS:

> Yeah, not those rich hipster imperialist
>
> tippets!

GEORGE:

> Oh, don't blame me, I didn't ask to sell this
>
> stuff!

JOOLS:

> Was that "You didn't ASK to sell this stuff?" or
> was it "You didn't ask to sell this STUFF"

GEORGE:

> Eh?

JOOLS:

> Oh nothing a bag of sad fish tears, then.

ROGERS:

> Make it two.

JOOLS:

> Oh, didn't realise you liked them. *[Shrug form ROGERS]* Two.

ROGERS:

> Thanks, Jools.

GEORGE:

> Are you the Project Management Institute?

JOOLS:

> Fuck off!

GEORGE:

> What?

JOOLS:

> Project Management Institute, I ask ya! We're The Institute of Project Management! Project Management Institute, God!

ROGERS:

> Blighters...

GEORGE:

> Can I...join your group?

JOOLS:

No, piss off!

GEORGE:

I didn't want to sell this stuff, it's only a job! I
hate the line management as much as anybody!

All in PMI except GEORGE:

Ssch! Ssch! Ssch! Ssch! Ssch!

GEORGE:

Oh.

JUDITH:

Are you sure?

GEORGE:

Oh, dead sure. I hate the line managers already
from marketing through to finance.

JOOLS:

Listen! If you wanted to join the IPM, you need
many, many, many, many years experience on
implementation projects.

GEORGE:

I do!

JOOLS:

Oh, yeah, how much? Got any evidence to back it up.

GEORGE:

A lot! Can't tell you much of it cause of the non-disclosure agreements, but I have lots honest.

JOOLS:

Right, *[pause]* you're in.   Listen!   The only people we hate more than the Line Managers, are the fucking Project Management Institute.

JUDITH:

Splitters!

ROGERS:

And the Project Managers Association!

All in IPM except GEORGE:

Yeah!

All in IPM except GEORGE:

Yeah! Splitters!

STAN THE SCRUM:

And the Institute of Project Managers!

All in IPM except GEORGE:

Yeah! Splitters!

JOOLS:

What?

STAN THE SCRUM:

The Institute of Project Management. More like the Idiots of Project Management! Splitters!

JOOLS:

We are the Institute of Project Management!

STAN THE SCRUM:

Oh. I thought we were the International Institute of Project Management.

JOOLS:

International Institute! God...

ROGERS:

Whatever happened to the International Institute, Jools?

JOOLS:

He's over there.

All in IPM except GEORGE:

Splitter!

PETER TAYLOR:

....and that is how not to get fired for being a lazy project manager. In summary, when someone senior is around, LOOK REALLY, REALLY BUSY. I don' t mean your normal run of the mill busy. Like moaning about going from meeting to meeting and not having time for lunch or a wee. Let me stress that, as you can hear I am saying this in capitals and bold. Imagine it, go on close your eyes and when I say imagine the big huge bold capital letters REALLY, REALLY, REALLY BUSY.

PROJECT MANAGER I *[Elbowing his colleague]*:

Is that it? Absolutely dreadful!

PROJECT MANAGER II *[Waking from his hangover]*:

Huh. Where's the breakfast buffet? I need coffee.

PETER TAYLOR

I have been Peter Taylor, the Lazy Project Manager. Stay Lazy, and LOOK BUSY!

AUDIENCE:

[Applause and chants of You're Lazy! You just Stay in Bed! Lazy! Lazy!]

JOOLS:

Peace, brother! Ha-ha! What's your name?

GEORGE:

George......George Onaswell.

JOOLS:

We may have a small sub-project for you, George.

Seven

What Have Project Managers Ever Done for Us?

SCENE: The interior of Pronto a Mangiare, a darkened Italian coffee house with a very conspiratorial atmosphere, the air is filled hint of freshly ground Arabica beans and the chilled out sound of indiscriminate jazz, playing just on the edge of ones hearing so that you know its there but cannot distinguish what the tune actually is, but guaranteed to be in your head for the rest of the week.

EDDY (Head of Accounts) and **JULIA** (Head of Human Resource) sit in luxurious brown leatherette sofas at a table that's too low to use as a real table but too high to not be in the way of one's knees.

FRANK (Head of Marketing), dressed in Activist gear, black polar neck, tan chinos and a pair of "formal" sneakers, is leaning awkwardly over the table sketching on a folded out napkin that is so thin you can almost see the fake grain of the mahoganyish laminate below.

He is outlining the plan to other members of the extended management team of Grunnlings Assorted Fixings (est. 1843) Ltd, each perched on the edge of the sofas, all with Activists masks concealing the lower half of their face, some covered with cappuccino froth having forgotten they had them on, others still wearing their company ID badges, with youthful photos of when they still had hair.

The discussions turns to the how to deal with the diabolical and despotic new Head of the PMO, Amadeus Pilate. Having replaced the beloved previous Head of the PMO, Arthur Pendragon, he quickly tried to stamp his authority onto the way projects are governed, with actions that have created disquiet among the loyal middle management of Grunnlings Assorted Fixings (est. 1843).....

FRANK:

We get in through the new air conditioning system here... up through to the main atrium, with the poinsettia display and yucca here... and Pilate's Head of PMO Personal Assistant's office. You know that new keen George fella, always wanted to be a Project Manager apparently, bit weird, makes a good coffee though. When we've grabbed him, we inform Pilate using the all company email account: GRUN.ASSRT.FXNGS.EST1843.DIST.ALL.COMP.EVRY.ONE.@GAFL.ME therefore protecting our identity, to issue our demands. Any questions?

XERXES:

What exactly are the demands?

EDDY:

We're giving Pilate two days to dismantle the entire governance apparatus of the New Project Management Office (est. 2007) Imperialist State and if he doesn't agree immediately we destroy his credibility.

MATTHEWS:

> Send him on a Business Ethics course then, insist he presents summarised, 3 bullet point approach that can be applied across the organisation.

FRANK:

> Hide his project plans and then we'll post inaccurate milestone dates on slack and twitter every hour on the hour. So everyone will be changing priorities left, right and centre, that'll show him we're not to be trifled with.

XERXES:

> Frank, I think you mean a different email account than:
>
> GRUN.ASSRT.FXNGS.EST1843.DIST.COMP.EVRY.ONE.@GAFL.ME.
>
> Is that the one for the just the permanent employees. If you want the one for everyone it's different, I think it's:
> GRUN.ASSRT.FXNGS.EST1843.DIST.ALL.COMP.EVRY.ONE.@GAFL.ME.

FRANK:

> What? I dunno, we can just use either can't we.

XERXES:

> I suppose so, just thought I would mention it, just in case it was important.

FRANK:

> Oh!, OK, thanks for that. Where were we? Oh yea, our demands. Eddy?

EDDY:

> Yes Frank, we're also demanding a ten-foot alabaster statue of the Project Sponsor Julius Caesar with his tackle hanging out in reception.

JULIA:

> What? They'll never agree to that, Eddy.

EDDY:

> That's just a bargaining tool. And of course, we point out that they bear full responsibility when everyone chops and changes what they are doing due to the milestone date changes, and... that we shall not submit to compelling business cases.

ACTIVISTS:

> (Applause) No business cases!

EDDY:

> They've bled our operational budgets dry, with their benefits realisation monitoring. It's like they WANT us to be accountable for their project's efficiency gains or something. They've taken everything we had, not just from us, from our managers and from our managers' managers.

JULIA:

> And from our managers' managers' managers.

EDDY:

> Yep.

JULIA:

> And from our managers' managers' managers' managers.

EDDY:

> All right, Jools. Don't keep banging on. And what have they ever given us in return?

JULIA:

> The Kanban board.

EDDY:

> Oh yeah, yeah they gave us that. Yeah. That's true.

MASKED ACTIVIST:

> And budgetary control!

JULIA:

> Oh yes... budgetary control, you remember what the company project spending used to be like.

EDDY:

> All right, I'll grant you that the Kanban board and the budgetary control are two things that the Project Managers have done...

MATTHEWS:

> And the risk management ...

EDDY: (sharply)

> Well yes, obviously the risk management, [pause] the risk management goes without saying, what kind of project management process would be without the risk management. Apart from the Kanban board, the budgetary control and the risk management...

ANOTHER MASKED ACTIVIST:

> Quality Management...

OTHER MASKED VOICES:

> Change Control... communication strategy... stakeholder analysis...

EDDY:

Yes... all right, fair enough...

ACTIVISTS:

And the Gantt charts...

NORMAN:

Oh yes! True!

FRANK:

Yeah. That's something we'd really miss if Project Managers left, Jools.

MASKED ACTIVIST AT BACK:

Daily stand-ups! Done my back the world of good they have.

JULIA:

And it's safe to go into the IT department now.

FRANK:

Yes, they certainly know how to keep those techies in check and delivering what we asked for instead of the latest technological wonder that in vogue at the minute....(general nodding)... let's face it, they're the only ones who translate what the hell they are talking about down there in the basement.

NORMAN:

> You're right their Frank, do you remember last year, I asked them to change the colour on one of the screens and I got a bill for 50 Amazon Echoes for the whole site, and an Alexa skill that allowed you to change the screen colour with my voice, which also dimmed the lights in the canteen. I only wanted it a shade less bright cause it was giving me a migraine.

MASKED ACTIVISTS:

> *[more general murmurs of agreement]*

EDDY *[red in the face with frustration, his voice rising in volume with each word, and spittle flying from his lips]*:

> OK, apart from the Kanban board, budgetary control and the risk management, quality management, controlling those bloody techies, change control, and all that other crap you just mentioned. What have those bastard Project Managers ever done for us? Eh?

GRUNNLINGS ASSORTED FIXINGS (EST. 1843) EXTENDED MANAGEMENT TEAM *[nervously considering this question, sensing EDDY'S tone]*:

> Rhubarb, rhubarb, rhubarb.

NEWLY[PROMOTED AND KEEN MEMBER OF THE EXTENDED MANAGEMENT TEAM *[meekly whispers]*:

> P..p..p..project Success?

EDDY *[very angry, his meeting is not going the way he wanted at all, he's not even sure who's taking the minutes]*:

> What!? Oh... (scornfully) Project Success .... oh sod off!

Eight

Always Look on the Bright Side of Project Life

SCENE: Our hero, George Onaswell, having come up against his first project business case rejection at the hands of the fearsome Grunnlings Assorted Fixings (est. 1843) Ltd Business Case Approval Board (est. 1996), stands, head down in the queue of shame with an old grizzled but cheery Project Director.

PROJECT ACCOUNTANT:
> Funded or Cancelled?

PROJECT MANAGER I:
> Cancelled.

PROJECT ACCOUNTANT:
> OK, first on the right down to explain yourself
> to all your stakeholders. They will be in, in a
> minute.

OLD GRIZZLED PROJECT DIRECTOR:
> Hiya!

PROJECT ACCOUNTANT:
> Hi. funded or cancelled

OLD GRIZZLED PROJECT DIRECTOR:
> Funded finally.

PROJECT ACCOUNTANT:
> Oh! Great! Not many of those today. You've been at
> this one for a while haven't you? Let's see,
> you're on version 93.6.a.iiiv. Wow, that has been
> a while. Well, off you go to tell your team the
> good news then.

OLD GRIZZLED PROJECT DIRECTOR:
> Nah! Only joking, cancelled again.

PROJECT ACCOUNTANT:
> You! You get me every time, don't you? You know
> the drill down to the right...

OLD GRIZZLED PROJECT DIRECTOR:
> ..first on the right wait outside.

PROJECT ACCOUNTANT:

Oh, you're new. Funded or Cancelled

GEORGE:

Cancelled.

PROJECT ACCOUNTANT:

OK, so follow the joker first on the right down to explain yourself to all your stakeholders. They will be in in a minute.

GEORGE [*proceeds down the corridor and take a seat next to the OLD GRIZZLED PROJECT DIRECTOR*]:

What am I gonna do now?

OLD GRIZZLED PROJECT DIRECTOR:

You'll be alright, let me tell you a few things about a project managers life.

[*The Old Grizzled Project Director jumps to his feet and bursts into song*]

Some things in projects are bad,

Project updates can really make you mad,

Budgeting just makes you swear and curse,

When your schedule is superficial,

Don't re-plan, give a whistle,

And pop out to Starbucks for a latte and a rest ...

And......always look on the bright side of project

life...

[Whistle]

Always look on the light side of project life...

[Whistle]

If project status seems jolly rotten,

There's opportunities that will be spot on,

to help you rescue slipping milestones on your plan,

When your risks are in the dumps,

your arms bristle with goosebumps,

Just take a deep breath and switch to agile and

Kanban,

And......always look on the bright side of project

life...

[Whistle]

Come on.

Always look on the right side of project life...

[Whistle]

For projects are quite absurd,

And close-down's the final word,

You must always face the project board with a bow,

Forget about your overrun sin,

give your sponsor an enormous grin,

Enjoy it, it's your last chance anyhow.

So always look on the bright side of your budget...

[Whistle]

a-Just before you have to terminally fudge it...

[Whistle]

Your plan's a piece of shit,

when you look at it

Your plan's a laugh and your budgets a joke, it's true

You'll see it's all a salesman show,

keep 'em approving as you go

Just think when the brown stuff hits the fan,

it lands on you,

And......Always look on the bright side of project

life...

[Whistle]

Always look on the right side of project life...

C'mon PM, cheer up,

Always look on the bright side of project life...

Always look on the bright side of project life...

Worse things happen in line management you know.

I mean – you've got nuffin to lose,

You know, you come from no scope,

you're going back to no scope.

What have you lost? Nuffin.

Always look on the right side (I mean) of project life...

what have you got to lose?

You know, you come from no funding,

you're going back to no funding.

What have you lost?

Always (Nothing.) look on the right side of project

life...

Nowt will come from nowt,

ya know what they say?

Cheer up ya old bugga,

c'mon give us a smile!

There ya are, see!

Always look on the risky side of project life...

(Cheer up ya old bugga c'mon give us a smile!

There ya go, see!

OLD GRIZZLED PROJECT DIRECTOR:

> Right, I have to be off, think this might be the
> last meeting I have with my programme board.
> Lol. That means laugh out loud you know.

GEORGE:

> Yeah, I know. Good luck.

OLD GRIZZLED PROJECT DIRECTOR:

> You too.

The Old Grizzled Project Director heads into the

meeting room whistling. George find himself

involuntarily whistling too and feeling a little bit

better.

Nine

I'm a Scrum Master

SCENE: The head office of Grunnlings Assorted Fixings (Est. 1843) Ltd, an office desk, at 10pm strewn with multiple, heavily branded, re-useable, insulated coffee cups. Behind a pile of partly stamped coffee shop loyalty cards, mainly for shops that went bust many months ago, our hero George Onaswell slowly wakes. He lifts his head from the half-eaten pizza, one slice stubbornly sticking to his left cheek. As it drops it leaves behind a circle of pepperoni, perfectly placed to resemble a clown's make-up. He stares into the distance and shakes his head forlornly.

I never really wanted to do this Project Manager job in the first place!

I... I wanted to be...

A Scrum Master!

(piano vamp)

Leaping from Scrum team to Scrum team! As they Sprint down towards the mighty Retrospectives the Agile Project British Columbia! With my SCRUM guide in my hand!

The Product Owner!

The Sprint Planning!

The Sprint Backlog!

The Daily Scrum!

The Definition of Done!

We'd sing! Sing! Sing!

Oh, I'm a Scrum Master, and the velocity is okay,

I Sprint all night and do Stand-ups each day.

CHORUS:

I'm a Scrum Master, and the velocity is okay,

I Sprint all night and do Stand-ups each day.

I remove impediments, I eat my lunch,

I run 15-minute Scrums daily.

On Wednesdays, I go reportin'

And the Scrum teams deliver products iteratively.

Mounties: He removes impediments, he eats his lunch,

He runs 15-minute Scrums dai-ly.

On Wednesdays 'e goes reportin'

And the Scrum teams deliver products iteratively.

CHORUS

I cut down impediments, I scrum and sprint,

I like to debug code.

I compile my latest routines,

And renovate classic cars.

Mounties: He removes impediments, he scrums and

sprints,

He likes to debug code.

He compiles his latest routines

And renovates .... classic cars???????

CHORUS

I chop down blockages, I wear a Marvel t-shirt

sandals with socks,

I wish I'd been a coder

Just the same as my old pops.

Mounties: he chops down blockages, he wears a Marvel

t-shirts,

Sandals??????? with .... socks????

(spoken, raggedly) What's that? Wants to be a "coder"?

Oh, goodness!

And I thought you were so agile! Techie!

CHORUS

All: He's a Scrum Master, and his velocity is

Okaaaaaaaaay..... (BONG)

Ten

Bring Me Green Status

Bring me green status, in your smile,

No red risks all the while,

In this project where we live,

there should be more agileness,

So much joy you can give,

to each, new, weekly, update.

Make me happy, through no delays,

Never bring me, I missed deliverays,

Let your RAGS be as green,

as the reception aspidistra high above

Bring me fun,

bring me green status,

bring me love.

Bring me green status, in your eyes

Bring me milestones,

bang on time

Life's too short to be spent,

having any status but green,

Our project sponsor will be,

less grumpy and not so mean.

Stay light-hearted,

in project boards,

Smiley faces,

on the dashboard,

Let your RAGS be as green,

as the reception aspidistra high above

Bring me fun,

bring me green statuses,

bring me love!

Eleven

I am Considerably Better Qualified than Him

SCENE: Three project manages stand next to each other in a line facing us, each certified from a different certification body.

PROJECT MANAGEMENT PROFESSIONAL (PMP) [*In bowler hat, black jacket and pinstriped trousers*]:

> I look down on him [*indicating the PMQ*] because I have a global project management certification.

ASSOCIATION OF PROJECT MANAGEMENT (PMQ) [*Pork-pie hat and raincoat*]:

> I look up to him [*PMP*] because his certification is global, but I look down on him [*PRINCE II*] because his certification does not have a Body of Knowledge. I am a middle-class project manager.

PRINCE II PRACTITIONER [*Cloth cap and muffler*]:

> I know my place. I look up to them both. But I don't look up to him [*PMQ*] as much as I look up to him [*PMP*], because he has got demonstrable experience.

PMP:

> I have got demonstrable experience, but I have not have a UK qualification. So sometimes I look up [*bends knees*] to him [*PMQ*].

PMQ:

> I still look up to him [*PMP*] because although I have a UK qualification, I do not have years of

validated experience. But I am not as un-validated as him [PRINCE II] so I still look down on him *[PRINCE II]*.

PRINCE II:

I know my place. I look up to them both; but while I do not have a professional certification, I have templates and industrialised, trusted procedures. Had I the inclination, I could look down on them, as they for not have the tools of the trade. But I don't.

PMQ:

We all know our place, but what do we get out of it?

PMP:

I get a feeling of superiority over them.

PMQ:

I get a feeling of inferiority from him, (PMP), but a feeling of superiority over him (PRINCE II).

PRINCE II:

I get a pain in the back of my neck.

ACCOUNTANT ACCA *[walking past]*:

I am a Chartered Accountant, I look down on all of them as they are not "professionals".

Twelve

12 Days of the Project

SCENE: It's 10:15pm, Christmas Eve and our hero George sits in the offices of Grunnlings Assorted Fixings (est. 1843) Ltd putting the final touches to his latest project status report. The deadline for the reports is always a Tuesday and no public holidays get in the way a status report. George looks out the his office windows at the flakes of snow, slowly and steadily drifting to the pavement below. Through the 2cm gap in the window a sound reaches his ears, he knows the tune well and begins to sing to himself.

On the **FIRST** day of the project, my sponsor gave to me

A fictional benefits case

On the **SECOND** day of the project, my sponsor gave to

me

Two backlog items

And a fictional benefits case

On the **THIRD** day of the project, my sponsor gave to me

Three full sprints

Two backlog items

And a fictional benefits case

On the **FOURTH** day of the project, my sponsor gave to

me

Four calling clients

Three full sprints

Two backlog items

And a fictional benefits case

On the **FIFTH** day of the project, my sponsor gave to me

FIVE GANTT CHARTS

Four calling clients

Three full sprints

Two backlog items

And a fictional benefits case

On the **SIXTH** day of the project, my sponsor gave to me

Six scopes a-creeping

FIVE GANTT CHARTS

Four calling clients

Three full sprints

Two backlog items

And a fictional benefits case

On the **SEVENTH** day of the project, my sponsor gave to
me

Seven risks red ragging

Six scopes a-creeping

FIVE GANTT CHARTS

Four calling clients

Three full sprints

Two backlog items

And a fictional benefits case

On the **EIGHTH** day of the project, my sponsor gave to me

Eight budgets a-busting

Seven risks red ragging

Six scopes a-creeping

FIVE GANTT CHARTS

Four calling clients

Three full sprints

Two backlog items

And a fictional benefits case

On the **NINTH** day of the project my sponsor gave to me

Nine milestones slipping

Eight budgets a-busting

Seven risks red ragging

Six scopes a-creeping

FIVE GANTT CHARTS

Four calling clients

Three full sprints

Two backlog items

And a fictional benefits case

On the **TENTH** day of the project, my sponsor gave to me

Ten issues escalating

Nine milestones slipping

Eight budgets a-busting

Seven risks red ragging

Six scopes a-creeping

FIVE GANTT CHARTS

Four calling clients, Three full sprints, Two backlog
items, And a fictional benefits case

On the **ELEVENTH** day of the project, my sponsor gave to me

Eleven planers planning

Ten issues escalating

Nine milestones slipping

Eight budgets a-busting

Seven risks red ragging

Six scopes a-creeping

FIVE GANTT CHARTS

Four calling clients

Three full sprints

Two backlog items

And a fictional benefits case

On the **TWELFTH** day of the project, my sponsor gave to me

Twelve retrospectives retrospecting

Eleven planers planning

Ten issues escalating

Nine milestones slipping

Eight budgets a-busting

Seven risks red ragging

Six scopes a-creeping

FIVE GANTT CHARTS

Four calling clients

Three full sprints

Two backlog items

[BIG FINISH]

AND A FICTIONAL BENEFITS

CAAAAAAAAAAAAAAAAAASE!

Dedication

To my beautiful wife and daughters who have no idea what I do for a living. They have as much knowledge as the characters in Friends do about Chandler's job. So I just say I am a transponster.

Also By Nigel Creaser

When I Were a Project Manager

Where it all began.

Are you a new project manager wondering what life might be like at the end of your career, maybe reminiscing about the journey with colleagues? Do you want a tiny glimpse into your future? Are you an accomplished project manager who recognises the funny stuff in the life of a project manager?

Well, this is the book for you! A parody of the "Four Yorkshiremen" sketch adapted for the project management community.

Peter Taylor, author of The Lazy Project Manager says:

> *"Python meets Project Manager! As a Monty Python fan and Lazy Project Manager, I just loved this excellent reworking"*

Available in digital and physical format in all the usual outlets.

The Sunday Lunch Project

George Onaswell is a typical Project Manager, been delivering projects for years, adept stakeholder manager and Gantt chart guru, then he gets the most terrifying high profile project of his career!

Cooking Sunday lunch for his prospective mother-in-law, head of the local Women's Institute and national roast dinner of the year champion four years on the trot.

How can he make it a roaring success while still delivering the thorny project he just got landed in the office?

The project charter is drafted for . . . .

The Sunday Lunch Project!!!

What could possibly go wrong?

In all good bookstores (and rubbish ones) in 2019 (...or in that general regionish)

About the Author

Nigel Creaser, PMP, PMQ, PSM, 25MSB[1] is an experienced project and programme manager with over 20 years of varied project management roles delivering multi-million pound projects across a wide range of industries including national and regional government, financial services and telecoms. He is a former Director of Marketing for the UK Chapter of the Project Management Institute, or was that the Management Institute Of Projects. Oi! Who said splitter?

He lives in North Shropshire with his wife and two daughters. When he is not managing projects or being a husband and dad, you can find him on a judo mat trying to stay standing or running around trying to get a bit faster and running a little bit further.

[1] 25 metre swimming badge.

Printed in Great Britain
by Amazon

62978141R00073